The Only Way is Ethics

Living Out My Story

And some pastoral and missional thoughts
about homosexuality along the way

Sean Doherty

T0385328

21 20 19 18 17 16 15   7 6 5 4 3 2 1

First published 2015 by Authentic Media Limited,
52 Presley Way, Crownhill, Milton Keynes, MK8 0ES.
authenticmedia.co.uk

British Library Cataloguing in Publication Data
A catalogue record for this book is available from the British Library.
ISBN: 978-1-78078-147-1   978-1-78078-436-6 (e-book)

Cover design by Sara Garcia

I became a Christian in my mid-teens. Not long afterwards, I came to recognise that I was gay.[1] Of course, today we are used to hearing that sexuality is a spectrum. Many people are in between the homosexual and heterosexual poles. But in my case, at least, my sexual attractions were firmly and exclusively oriented towards other men. At the time, identifying myself as gay was just a simple and natural description of who I was and how I felt.

So, homosexuality is not at all a theoretical issue for me (not that it is for anyone). It is a journey I have walked, mostly joyfully, occasionally painfully, always knowing that God was present within it. I want to tell you my story first, so I have saved the theological and biblical stuff for later. That means some of the things I say now will assume the arguments I set out later (feel free to read ahead if you prefer). But I felt it was important to start with my personal journey.

As a teenager and then a student, I attended evangelical churches which taught and explained what I will call the 'classic' Christian understanding of sex and marriage – namely that sex is a good gift from God but it is a gift that God has given for marriage (and, we must now add, that marriage is between a woman and a man). Not that this view was forced on me – wise and supportive mentors

_____

[1] I'll talk later about whether that was the best word to use, but it was the one I used at the time.

encouraged me to read about the subject and to work out what I thought for myself. As a theology undergraduate, I took the opportunity to look at different views and interpretations. I continued to be convinced that sex was indeed a good gift for marriage, and that recent attempts to find exceptions to this were not convincing. To my mind, the classic teaching of the Church about sex was indeed the biblical and authentic Christian one, and so I committed myself to celibacy.

At university, I was open about being gay and celibate amongst Christians and non-Christians alike, and I never experienced homophobic treatment from evangelical Christians – although I was at times scorned or pitied by non-Christians and a few liberal Christians for being celibate. For me, the church was my safe place: far from being ostracised, I was nurtured there, given opportunities to preach, and encouraged to consider whether God might be calling me to ordination. I was a member of the prayer ministry and worship teams of my church, and the exec of my Christian Union (CUs are not normally bastions of radical liberal theological sentiment). The other exec members, who knew about my sexuality, treated me with nothing but respect and affection.

In my experience at least, Christians who believe that same-sex activity was sinful were not homophobic. The issue is what you do, not your orientation. Unconditional love and acceptance of a person does not imply unconditional approval of everything they do. Such love and acceptance was my consistent experience.

Tragically, the church has not always treated gay people so well. Some people have been held back from ministry and even excluded from baptism and communion simply because of their sexual orientation, regardless of whether they were sexually active or not. Some have been insulted and mistreated – whereas the Bible commands us to treat people with 'gentleness and respect' (1 Pet. 3:15).[2]

So there is homophobia in the church, although not necessarily more than in any other context. But in my experience, it is undeniable that there is also love and unconditional acceptance of gay people just as we are. Homophobia is an irrational hatred of gay people based simply on the fact that we are gay. But I experienced no 'irrational hatred', even though I was in an environment which taught that sex was only for marriage between a man and a woman. Indeed, that was what I believed too. And I did not have irrational hatred of myself. Believing that gay sex is not right is not the same as irrationally hating or fearing gay people. Homophobia can coexist with the view that gay sex is wrong, but this view does not cause homophobia. We must confront and challenge real homophobia, and there is enough of that to deal with, without pretending that classic Christian convictions about sexual morality are inherently homophobic.

Single and celibate

So I had accepted myself as gay and decided to be celibate, and in church I had been both accepted for who

---

[2]For example, see Wesley Hill, 'The Church is Homophobic – True or False?' at http://spiritualfriendship.org/2014/01/31/the-church-is-homophobic-true-or-false/.

I was, and supported to live celibately. I never tried to change my sexual orientation, although I did pray a few times that my orientation would change. When it did not, I felt it was right to leave it at that, as in the example of Paul with his 'thorn in the flesh' in 2 Corinthians 12:7–9. Whatever this thorn was (we don't really know – perhaps a chronic physical ailment), Paul asked God 'three times' to take it away. His first assumption was that God would intervene. And I absolutely believe that God can and does at times intervene to bring about miraculous transformation (not just in our sexualities). But in my case there was not (and still has not been) any miraculous change in my feelings. Paul's example was very helpful in teaching me that God can be present in the challenges we face, not just in overcoming them. Indeed, his power is not only present in our weakness but 'made perfect' in it (verse 9).

There were advantages to thinking I would remain single. I didn't have to wonder if there was someone out there for me, or spend time looking for them. I had to face squarely the likelihood that I would not share my life with a specific companion, have sexual intimacy with another person or have children. I could grieve for these things – whereas many single people find the perpetual uncertainty as to whether they will marry or not very hard. Instead, I channelled my attention into living as well as I could as a single person – in particular, cultivating friendships, and growing in my relationship with God.

Singleness inevitably brought challenges too. There were times of loneliness. I have wonderful friends and close family, yet from time to time I especially missed having a 'special someone' who was there just for me. This has led me to believe that (like Jesus and his disciples), everyone needs these kinds of intentional, special friendships with others, even though only marriage should be the place for a sexual relationship.

Occasionally I developed feelings for particular guys that I knew. I was lucky in the sense that I never fell deeply in love with another man, but a couple of times it was hard to realise I had feelings for guys (based on the desire for intimacy and closeness rather than on physical attraction), and to choose not to act on them. I found it easier not to tell them, although others in similar situations have found it more helpful to talk to the person (or at least to someone who knows them both) in order to be accountable and clear the air.

Despite these challenges, on the whole I was pretty peaceful about my sexual orientation, and the prospect of remaining celibate. But you may have heard the joke: 'How do you make God laugh? Tell him your plans.' I assumed that celibacy was the cross I had to bear, that it would be permanent, because sexual orientation is permanent – isn't it? God had surprises in store!

Opening up to God's plans

Looking back now, I would say that I had put God and myself in a box. Because of my orientation, I had made assumptions about what God might and might not do in my life. And I had put myself into a box by assuming that my sexual desires would never change. This led me almost to idolise my celibacy, in the sense that I let it define me.

Over time, God changed a number of things about the
way I understood my sexual orientation, and therefore my
identity.

First, I realised that it was up to God whether I remained
single, not me. By focusing on my orientation, I had drawn
my own conclusions about the way life would pan out. But
God's purpose in our lives often unfolds gradually. Usually, God does not tell us everything in advance! Whilst
much of God's general will for our lives is set out in Scripture, we discover his specific will for our particular callings
as individuals, families, churches and so on along life's
way. (Of course, that must accord with Scripture.) Focus-
sing on myself, on my orientation, meant I had not waited
for God's voice afresh at each stage. Yet I tried to listen to
God and discern God's will in other areas of my life. The
crucial shift was doing this with my sexuality and celibacy
too. I started to be more open and less certain about what
God's will would be for that part of my life.

Alongside this was a growing sense that God was
actually interested in my sexuality. God cared about it,
wanted to work in it. Although it was right to surrender my sexuality to God's will by abstaining from sexual
activity, surrender on its own was not sufficient. Whilst
there was no guarantee that God would transform my
sexual desires, I came to believe that God was able and
willing to do so.

As I look back on this stage of my journey, I find the
work of psychologist William F. Kraft very illuminat-
ing (although I hadn't read it at the time). He argues
that many of us assume that the only two ways of

handling sexual desire are repression and gratifica-
tion.[3] But both of these are unhealthy! It is true that there are
many times when we should not indulge sexual desire, but
this does not mean we must repress it. Kraft argues that we
can instead *suppress* it, which means accepting your feelings
without choosing to promote or act on them. This was true
for me: I had not sought to deny my sexuality. I accepted my
orientation and myself but did not act on my desires.

But, Kraft says, even suppression is, ideally, only one
stage along a journey towards integration.[4] For me,
this meant letting God into my sexuality – even into my
unwanted desires, so that God could do what God wanted
with them. I already accepted that God loved me just as
I was – a central gospel truth. But there is another central
gospel truth: whilst God loves us just as we are, God also
loves us enough not to leave us that way.

So, here were two key insights: I had to keep listening
to God and not assume I would stay on the path I had
been expecting; God had the power and desire to bring
change (or integration) to my sexuality. But the third and
final shift was the most important one.

Identity rather than orientation

The most important shift in the way I saw myself was a
change in how I saw my sexual identity. This change took

---

[3]William F. Kraft, *Whole and Holy Sexuality: How to Find Human and Spiritual Integrity as a Sexual Person* (Eugene, OR: Wipf and Stock, 1989), p. 83.
[4]*Whole and Holy Sexuality*, p. 90 onwards.

place in a theology lecture I happened to attend. The lecturer asked the rhetorical question, 'Did God create four sexes?' My brain automatically supplied the answer: no. God did not create straight women, straight men, gay women and gay men. God created two sexes, with the capacity to relate to one another sexually. In other words, I had regarded my sexual orientation as what defined my sexual identity. It determined whether I could get married or not. But the Bible, as the lecturer's words reminded me, defines sexuality in much more earthy, physical and bodily terms: 'male and female he created them' (Gen. 1:27). I realised that my sexual identity was not discerned in my sexual desires but in the plain, tangible fact that I am a man. Thus, as a man, God's original intention for me in creation was to be able to relate sexually to a woman (not that all women and men will be called to relate sexually to someone of the opposite sex). This was still true, even though currently my sexual feelings did not match it. This opened up for me the possibility of marriage.

This takes a bit of explaining in a culture that places such a strong emphasis on being true to our feelings. When constructing our sexual identity, we tend to emphasise our feelings: they define with whom we might or might not form a healthy relationship. I was a typical example of this: having a same-sex *orientation* immediately led to a conclusion about my sexual *identity*. There was no shame in that identity – perhaps because of our general cultural attitude now, or because my parents never regarded homosexuality as problematic. Identifying as gay was a simple acknowledgement of my orientation. But, gradually,

I came to believe that in fact it was my feelings that were relatively superficial, in comparison to my physical identity. It is not that sexual feelings are unimportant according to the Bible, but they should not define us.

What this meant for me was that without denying or ignoring my sexual feelings I stopped regarding them as being who I was, and started regarding my body as defining my sexual identity. I felt God calling me to stop identifying myself as gay – even though at this stage I had not experienced any change in my sexual orientation. When I stopped identifying myself as gay, I *did* experience some change – enough that subsequently I fell in love with and eventually married Gaby, who had been a good friend for several years.

The overall pattern of my sexual desires has not changed. I am still predominantly same-sex attracted. In a sense it has ceased to matter to me whether I am attracted to women or men in general. But it matters a great deal that I am attracted to my wife! Of course, nearly all married people are attracted to other people at times. But marriage is about being attracted and called to be faithful to one person in particular, and our marriage is certainly a happy and fulfilling one. We face our share of challenges, but they are usually things such as tidying the house, juggling work with family commitments, and how grumpy I feel in the mornings, and hardly ever about sex!

Why gay people feel so marginalised by the church

My experience helps explain (although it does not magically solve) the massive pressure inside and outside the church to change our moral teaching to fit contemporary views about same-sex relationships. Since in our culture we tend to define sexual identity by sexual feelings, no wonder lesbian and gay people (as a group) feel marginalised and excluded by the church. Church teaching on sex and marriage means that gay people feel excluded de facto from marriage, many forms of family life, sexual intimacy and so on. If being gay precludes you from marrying someone of the opposite sex, then being gay means no sex, no children of your own, and no intimate companionship.

But my experience shows that it is the combination of Christian teaching on sex with the very recent assumption that your sexual attractions define you which causes this. It is not the conviction that sex is only for (opposite-sex) marriage that causes an injustice but the assumption that some people are inherently excluded from marriage simply by being who they are. In our society now, the presumed solution to the injustice this creates is to dismantle classic Christian sexual morality. But my experience calls into question the idea that some people are inherently excluded from marriage by their sexuality. The dominant view of sexual identity today is an incredibly recent development. If we have to choose between this development and the classic Christian interpretation of Scripture, it is not obvious to me why we should ditch the latter. I found it freeing to doubt contemporary assumptions about sexual identity. This opened new possibilities to me, and enabled me to accept myself more fully as I am, that is, physically. Rather than downplaying the significance of our actual bodies, and far from being anti-body and anti-sex, the traditional Christian view acknowledges the goodness of our bodies as male or female, rather than subordinating them to our sexual orientation when it comes to defining sexual identity.

Mark Yarhouse, whose work we shall look at more closely below, therefore argues that we should distinguish between sexual *attraction* (a general description of feelings), sexual *orientation* (a strong and persistent pattern of sexual feelings), and sexual *identity* (a person's understanding of themselves).[5]

What is real homophobia, and how can we prevent it?

According to Stonewall, homophobia is 'the irrational hatred, intolerance, and fear of lesbian, gay and bisexual people'.[6] That is, homophobia is negative feelings or treatment of someone based purely on our sexuality, rather than because of anything we might do about it. But being gay is no more sinful than being straight. Both orientations involve sexual temptation and attractions to people outside opposite-sex marriage (unless there are a few holy and very unusual people out there who

[5]Mark Yarhouse, *Homosexuality and the Christian* (Bloomington, MN: Bethany House, 2010), pp. 41–2. See also Andrew Goddard and Don Horrocks, *Resources for Church Leaders: Biblical and Pastoral Responses to Homosexuality* (London: Evangelical Alliance, 2012), pp. 25–8.
[6]See 'What is homophobia', online at http://www.stonewall.org.uk/at_home/sexual_orientation_faqs/2697.asp.

have only ever been attracted to their spouse). The reality is that everyone's sexual desires are distorted by sin, and we all need God's forgiveness. So, on the whole it is absolutely essential to treat gay people just like anyone else. Homophobia is treating us differently because of our sexuality.

Let me give you a couple of real examples. A church with a number of attendees who were cohabiting with their (opposite sex) partner did not allow them to take a public leadership role within the church because they were in a sexual relationship outside marriage. They recognised that the Christian view is not that sex is for a man and a woman as such but that it is for opposite-sex marriage. By contrast, another church discovered that one of its male leaders was sleeping with his girlfriend but took no action, yet they did not allow a gay person who was seeking to live a celibate life to be involved in children's ministry. (What makes this even worse is the prejudice that a gay person is also more likely to be a paedophile, whereas of course they are entirely separate.) Whether you agree with these specific boundaries or not, one church was consistent and the other was not. It is homophobic to treat gay or same-sex oriented people differently to the way you treat straight people.

One particularly dangerous form of homophobia is so-called 'jokes' and negative generalisations about gay people. This is deeply damaging, spiritually and psychologically. It can make us feel ashamed of who we are and make it harder for us to believe that God loves us. It certainly makes it harder for us to talk openly about our sexuality and thereby find acceptance and support. One celibate guy I know was on the verge of coming out to his pastor, when his pastor joked about something being 'gay'. He was devastated and no longer felt able to talk to his pastor, isolating him at a time when he most needed encouragement and love. If you are serious about gay people trusting and feeling safe in church, it is crucial to cut out these behaviours from your life, and to challenge them in others, inviting them to repent where appropriate.

Given that many LGBT+ people have been hurt by the church, how can we make sure they feel welcome and accepted?

A friend who is a vicar rang me up to ask for advice: 'Sean, a gay couple have started coming to my church. What should I do?'

I replied, 'Have you tried offering them a cup of tea?'

This reply might seem absurdly simplistic (and I did go on to say more than that). My point was simply that gay people aren't different. We have the same basic human needs as anyone else: to be welcomed warmly and hospitably, to be accepted as we are – and to meet with Jesus. In one important way, we should not think that the situation of LGBT+ people is different to anyone else's, just because of our sexuality.

But because of the way that some LGBT+ people have been treated by the church, and because of the extremely negative media picture of the church with respect to sexuality, many gay people are wary of church and Christianity.

Understandably, they do not want to be hurt too, or hurt again.

If a gay person or couple comes to your church, or if someone comes out to you, in itself that is a fantastic start. They have taken a brave step and placed trust in you. Say that you are glad and grateful that they are there, and that they are welcome just as they are, although don't overdo it or be patronising. Apart from this, be normal. Get to know them, invite them for coffee, do whatever you'd do with anyone else – just basic decent treatment of a fellow human being.

As you get to know them more, ask them how much of their story and journey they want to share with you, and listen. This is always a privilege. If they have been hurt in the past, acknowledge this and take it seriously. Ask them what they would find helpful, or if there is anything you can to do to make things safe and welcoming for them (everyone's different).

I heard a great example of this recently. A gay couple wanted to do an evangelistic course at a church, and they let the church know that they would be coming as a couple. Rather than plunging into chapter and verse about the Bible and sexuality, the pastor invited them for dinner. Without setting aside what he believed, he said that they would be completely welcome. He realised they were taking a brave step, and he asked if there was anything he could do to help ensure they felt welcomed. He asked them to let him know if they encountered any homophobia from other participants on the course. In short, he demonstrated that they already had something to offer and teach him and the wider church.

But doesn't welcoming everyone mean endorsing their beliefs or choices?

God calls the church to welcome everyone, just as God welcomes every one of us 'while we were still sinners' (Romans 5:8). At work, in your neighbourhood, and perhaps in your family, you are already surrounded by people who do not share your beliefs about life, the universe and everything else. Even in church, you will know people with all sorts of different views about politics, ethics and Christian doctrine. Hopefully, you manage to get on with all these people, most of the time.

Imagine that at church you meet a cohabiting (opposite-sex) couple. If you become friends, and especially if one or both of them consider themselves to be Christians, there will come a point for a gentle but honest conversation about how their situation relates to following Christ and his teaching about sex and marriage. But you probably won't plunge into that when you first meet them, nor would it be the sole or dominant topic of your conversation.

It is essential to welcome, love and accept gay people in exactly the same way. They may believe and live differently to you. But there is nothing especially unusual about that. Treating people decently does not mean endorsing everything about them. Rather, welcoming people and treating them with love and respect strengthens the chances that they will meet with God, receive good teaching, and grow in maturity. Precisely by loving and accepting people just as they are, they will see something of God's love for them and surrender their lives more fully to God.

Our model here should be Jesus. He held various moral convictions, yet he responded quite differently to different individuals according to what they needed. Hence, he dramatically challenged the rich young ruler to sell everything, he saved the life of the woman caught in adultery, and told her she was not condemned before telling her not to sin any longer, and he exposed the adulterous hearts of the men who brought the woman to him. Holding our convictions without compromise doesn't mean that we must announce them at every opportunity. It means that we will treat the person in the way that they need so that they can meet with Jesus and be transformed.

If a gay person or same-sex couple start attending a church, their immediate need is almost certainly not to be confronted with the biblical teaching about sex. Of course, sex is something that church leaders should regularly teach on, as part of an ongoing balanced diet of good teaching. But we primarily need to be welcomed warmly, loved and accepted just as we are, and offered a safe environment in which to grow in our faith – precisely to help us live according to biblical teaching.

Should people try to change their sexuality?

There is relatively little evidence either way as to whether efforts to change someone's sexuality through psychotherapy are effective. Certainly, some people who have had this kind of therapy have experienced change – but in the absence of a 'control' group, it is impossible to prove whether or not the therapy caused the change.[7] What we can say for sure (against popular misconceptions) is that there is no sound scientific evidence that they are harmful. Indeed, some evidence suggests that they may benefit some participants, even those whose sexual orientation experiences no change.[8] Mark Yarhouse, part of the team who conducted the most substantial study so far of therapy and sexual orientation change, found that most of the positive benefits reported by people in his research 'were not about a dramatic change in sexual orientation. Rather, participants tended to emphasise their relationship with God, their experience of God's love and acceptance, and spiritual growth. That's not to say that change did not occur.'[9] He therefore believes that therapy is most helpful when the focus is not on changing one particular part of the person's feelings but on assisting them towards greater emotional and spiritual wholeness in general.

Yarhouse believes that the crucial thing to address in therapy is not someone's sexual feelings but their sexual identity – how they see themselves. My experience corroborates this. An important aspect of my journey was coming to believe that a significant part of me, namely my body, was genuinely already oriented towards the

---

[7] Some people experience fluctuations in their sexual attractions quite naturally over the course of their lifetimes, as we will see below.

[8] The best study is Stanton Jones and Mark A. Yarhouse, *Ex-Gays? A Longitudinal Study of Religiously Mediated Change in Sexual Orientation* (Downers Grove, IL: IVP Academic, 2007).

[9] *Homosexuality and the Christian*, p. 94.

possibility of (opposite-sex) marriage. My sexual identity as a man was already fixed and secure. So my primary need was not for my sexual desires to change but to recognise and welcome my existing identity as a good gift from God. The change I then experienced was a result of trusting in the good way God had made me. Rather than changing my feelings, so that I could change my label, I changed my label (or God did) and then my feelings started to follow.

This perspective is important in countering the assumption that straight is somehow normal and gay is not. If a person changes from widespread sexual desire towards people of the same sex to widespread sexual desire towards people of the opposite sex, that is not actually an improvement from a Christian perspective. 'Straight' should not be the goal as such but either fulfilled marriage or fulfilled singleness. So, whilst nobody (least of all people under the age of 18) should be pressurised, still less forced, to have any kind of psychotherapy where these are the goals, I think that people who have made an informed choice to have it should be free to do so.

Should Christians describe themselves as gay, straight, etc?

This touches on the question of whether I and other same-sex oriented Christians should call ourselves gay in the first place. As in my case, the term does not automatically imply an endorsement of same-sex sexual relationships. Similarly, author and theologian Wesley Hill identifies himself as gay but has been prominent in arguing that

Scripture rules out same-sex sexual relationships and advocating celibacy as a fulfilling way of life.[10] He and others, such as Julie Rodgers, have found the term helpful simply to describe their sexual orientation.[11]

Indeed, for me, identifying as gay was actually very helpful for a time, because it meant I was being honest about my orientation. It helped me accept myself as I was, and come to terms with what that meant for my life. These days, as I have said, I prefer not to use the term gay (not least because I am now married with children and it confuses people). This is not because I am ignoring or denying my sexual orientation but because I no longer regard it as the decisive marker of my sexual identity. Biblically speaking, I believe this should be defined in terms of male and female, not heterosexual or homosexual.

This is a point drawn out well by Christian anthropologist Jenell Williams Paris, who argues that the binary concepts of gay and straight can be marginalising and excluding. The term 'straight' is particularly problematic, because it was originally paired with 'bent', a pejorative term for gay people. In each class Paris teaches on sexuality, she therefore 'comes out' as being 'no longer heterosexual'.[12] This is not because she is gay but because 'straight' implies that there is something

---

[10]See Wesley Hill, *Washed and Waiting: Reflections on Christian Faithfulness and Homosexuality* (Grand Rapids, MI: Zondervan, 2010).

[11]See Julie Rodgers, 'Can the Gay be a Good?' online at https://julierodgers.wordpress.com/2014/10/23/can-the-gay-be-a-good/.

[12]Jenell Williams Paris, *The End of Sexual Identity: Why Sex is Too Important to Define Who We Are* (Downers Grove, IL: IVP, 2011), p. 43.

normal about heterosexuality, whereas in a fallen world, everybody's sexuality is equally broken. Sexually desiring many people of the opposite sex to whom you are not married is no better or worse than sexually desiring many people of the same sex. The norm is not straight but marriage or singleness.

It therefore seems preferable to me to eschew words such as gay, straight, homosexual, heterosexual, and so on. I am not sure how accurate these categories are as descriptions of the often complex and fluid nature of sexual desire anyway. But because the term gay itself does not imply a view one way or the other about sexual ethics, there is no absolute reason to avoid it. For some people, it will be helpful pastorally to use the term to describe themselves, whilst others find it more helpful not to define themselves in that way.

Then what about 'ex-gay' or 'healing' homosexuality?

For similar reasons, I would never describe myself as 'ex-gay'. This term makes it sound as if I have experienced more change in my sexual attractions than I really have. It would certainly be very nice if we all stopped experiencing temptation and only desired what was right. But God promises us the power to resist temptation, not to cease experiencing it. Jesus himself experienced temptation in every way that we do.

So, it is not necessary (or possible) to be free here and now of every disordered desire, sexual or otherwise. That will only happen when Jesus returns. Maybe some lucky people experience a total transformation of their sexual desires. I have never met one. But I do have the privilege of knowing many who remain entirely or predominantly same-sex attracted but who believe that their sexual identity is found in the fact that God has made them men or women. Some have become attracted to someone of the opposite sex and gone on to have fulfilling marriages, including sexually. Others, who have not fallen for anyone of the opposite sex, rightly remain single and therefore celibate. But someone who has moved beyond or never adopted the labels of 'gay' and 'straight', who does not define their sexuality in those terms, is not celibate because they are gay but because they are unmarried.

This redresses the profound sense of injustice caused by the perception that the Bible and the church call gay people to be celibate, whilst straight people don't have to be. First, it loosens the perceived connection between celibacy and homosexuality. Some supposedly gay people have normal and fulfilling opposite-sex marriages. Second, being gay isn't what means you should be celibate (as if gay is a special category of person) but rather being single. The playing field is levelled, because all people are called either to celibacy or marriage on the basis of their own particular vocation and situation in life, rather than by virtue of belonging to a particular sexual category.

I never speak of being 'healed' of homosexuality. This language is deeply damaging, because it loads shame onto people at the very deep level of their identity: they may feel told that there is something wrong with the very way that they are. Homosexuality is not an illness or a disease to be cured but rather a disordered desire. Nor is deliverance the answer, since the problem is not a demon. The biblical prescription, for me at least, was truth, the truth that my sexual identity is male, not gay. That was the truth which set me free (John 8:31–32).

Should people who are committed to the mainstream Christian teaching about sex and marriage attend a civil partnership ceremony or same-sex wedding?

This feels like a real catch-22. Assuming that the relationship is sexual (and not intentionally celibate), if you attend a civil partnership ceremony or same-sex wedding, you may feel that you are publicly endorsing the couple's decision to commit themselves to a lifelong sexual relationship which you believe is sinful. And if it's sinful, it's ultimately not best for them.

But if you politely decline to attend the ceremony, the couple (and probably others) will understandably be hurt. They have honoured you by offering you hospitality and inviting you to be part of their special day, especially if they know you are a Christian (most gay people know perfectly well what the usual Christian view is of same-sex relationships). If you don't attend, they may feel personally rejected by you, although you don't mean anything of the sort. You may come across as judgemental and homophobic. Worst of all, this may put some people off the church and therefore off Christ.

So, it seems to be a no-win situation. If you go, you may be sending a message that doesn't truly represent your beliefs. But if you don't go, you may also send a message that doesn't truly represent your beliefs. Whichever you do, you are liable to be misinterpreted.

My wife and I have attended more than one civil partnership ceremony. (We have not yet been invited to any same-sex weddings.) Because we recognised we were potentially going to send the wrong signal whatever we did, we decided that it was more important to show our friends the acceptance and unconditional love that we felt towards them personally, by accepting their offer of hospitality and being present with them. We would prefer people to form a wrong impression of what we think about their sexual ethics, than for them to misunderstand our care for them personally. Attending these ceremonies sought to show them our love and the fact that we valued our friendship.

In one case, neither partner was a practising Christian. Their primary need was to come to know Jesus. Although the gospel always involves repentance as well as faith, we felt that explaining our view of sexual ethics was not the main priority at this stage. Rather, we wanted to send them a strong signal that we care about and support them personally.

In another case, the couple were committed Christians who have reached a different theological view to us about same-sex relationships. They were to have a service of blessing for their relationship immediately following their civil ceremony. In this case, in fear and trembling I rang up one of them and thanked her for the honour of inviting us. I explained that we'd love to come to the civil ceremony but we felt we couldn't be present during the blessing. If it was hurtful or offensive to her (and I knew it could well be) then we would prefer not to come than to hurt them. She was extremely gracious, and encouraged us to come to the civil ceremony and quietly slip out before the blessing. This awkward and potentially hurtful kind of conversation will not always be appropriate, and we need wisdom in working out when to speak, and when to remain silent.

Of course, if somebody sincerely wants to know what you think, then you must give them a gentle but honest answer. But I don't think you should feel guilty or that you are undermining what you believe by attending. You *are* showing them something of your faith, namely that they are precious to God and to you. That is part of the gospel. Of course, the gospel is much more than that, but in the circumstances I think it's more important to show them the aspect of the gospel which they most need at this stage.

What about when someone becomes a Christian?

Our priority must be to accept gay people just as they are. Doing this is not soft-selling the gospel but an expression of it. Jesus accepted people just as they were. But as people met with Jesus, things started to change in their lives. Indeed, it was precisely Jesus's radical acceptance of sinners that transformed them. If a gay person or couple become Christians and start growing in their faith, their lives will change.

But we need to be wary of jumping to conclusions about how people will change and at what speed. We all have many issues in our lives, and God is gracious with us in terms of accepting us and changing us a bit at a time. God sometimes does stuff immediately. Usually, the process takes time.

One person I know, who was in a long-term same-sex relationship, became a Christian with his partner through the ministry of a prayer group. Over time, he felt God convince him that he needed to break up with his partner in order to refrain from sex outside marriage.[13] He broke the news to his partner, and they were both devastated. The next time he attended the prayer group (his partner did not attend), he asked for prayer because of the break-up. The group were astonished. They had not realised that they were a couple. If they had realised, and confronted them about it, my friend believes that he and his partner would have run a mile from them, and from God. Sometimes, God uses our silence. It is the Holy Spirit's job to convict the world of sin (John 16:8) – not our job.

Another friend and his partner became Christians and so far have continued to have a sexual relationship. But God is clearly at work in their lives. Right away, they fought to give up drugs, and experienced God's help in that struggle. More recently, my friend has felt God helping him to trust God with his business and financial situation – something many mature Christians still struggle with. I would obviously love them to lay down their sexual

---

[13] I don't believe that this is the only option for same-sex couples where one or both partners have become Christians, as I explain here: http://www.livingout.org/resources/celibate-same-sex-couples, and here: http://www.livingout.org/resources/becoming-christians-what-if-you-are-an-ssa-couple.

relationship as they grow in faith. But in the meantime, they are undeniably growing in other ways. And we have been able to have honest conversations without any of us having to change our views of sexual morality.

Of course, if someone exploring faith asks us an honest question about sexual morality, it is important not to bury anything in the small print.[14] When sharing the gospel with someone, it is essential to emphasise that becoming a Christian means taking up your cross to follow Christ, and God turning everything in your life upside down: your money, your career, your relationships. We must not mislead people into thinking that following Jesus means continuing with life in other respects just as before. At the same time, God is patient and may work within different aspects of our lives in different orders and at different times. When people become Christians, we need to give them good teaching, and some space to let God work. This is messy because God doesn't sort everything out overnight – but that is exactly the same with you and me. None of us is the finished article yet either.

What about more mature Christians who are not seeking to live according to biblical teaching?

Christians are called to admonish one another (Col. 3:16). It's quite right to gently encourage one another to follow

---

[14]Sam Allberry, quoted in Justin Brierley, 'A Different Kind of Coming Out' in *Christianity Magazine* (August 2013), online at http://www.premierchristianity.com/Past-Issues/2013/August-2013/A-Different-Kind-of-Coming-Out.

Christ more faithfully, which at times could certainly include directly discussing people's sexual morality with them and exhorting them to conform their lives to Jesus's teaching. But you must not single out Christians in same-sex relationships. It is very important to treat everyone consistently, whether with matters as weighty as baptism and communion, or as trivial as sharing a bedroom at a church weekend away or in your home. Do we do the same with, for example, greedy people, cohabiting couples, and people who gossip?

If you do decide to discuss sexuality with someone directly, it is rarely helpful to go in with all guns blazing. It's probably best to start by asking some open questions, and genuinely listening to what people say. Ask them how much of their story they feel comfortable sharing. Ask them how they relate their sexuality to their faith. Have they explored the current debates in the church for themselves? This will help you to understand how much they have engaged with the classic Christian teaching about sex. Some may never have heard it: knowing that something is generally supposed to be a sin is not at all the same as exploring and understanding the biblical story, its view of sex, and therefore the reasons for its prohibition of same-sex activity. You can help someone in this situation by gently introducing them to this fuller biblical picture, and walking with them as they explore it for themselves – reading, thinking, discussing, and praying.

It is important to be honest about the fact that there is more than one point of view in the church today on this issue – two minutes online and they will discover that for themselves anyway. It's much better to acknowledge this but explain which view you find convincing and why.

Many people have already gone through this process of exploration, and come to a different conclusion on the matter than the one set out here. For me, a helpful question to explore is why they have reached that conclusion. Is it based on an honest engagement with Scripture? That is, what is the real point of difference between you – the interpretation of Scripture or its authority? I often ask people, 'If I could show you that what you believe is not what the Bible says, would you change your mind?' I would indeed change my mind, if someone showed me that my view was not the biblical one. When I ask this question, very often the answer is, 'No.' In other words, the person has not ultimately reached their view on biblical grounds alone.

What about those in church leadership who are not seeking to live according to biblical teaching?

Although I have argued for a very welcoming, accepting approach towards gay people, the New Testament (especially 1 Tim. and Titus) is also clear that those involved in church leadership are called to lead lives in keeping with the church's teaching. Again, it is essential to be consistent and not to prevent some people from entering leadership whilst allowing others whose lives fall equally short. But someone who did not believe in certain core doctrines of the Christian faith would not expect to have a public leadership role in church, such as worship leading, preaching, administering communion and so on. As we will see, the classic Christian view about marriage and sex is not a peripheral, minor aspect of what Christians believe. It is related to and part of the doctrinal core of our faith. How we live is integrally related to what we believe.

Not that you can sort out everything in your life before you get involved in ministry. The key points, with any moral issue, would be for someone to recognise that it is an issue, to repent when they yield to temptation, to desire and seek to live according to Jesus's teaching, and to surrender that aspect of their life to him. That is very different to someone who flatly denies that some-thing is a temptation or issue in the first place. It's not about whether someone already has everything sorted out (none of us do) but about the direction in which they are heading.

Conclusion

I hope that sharing my own journey has demonstrated that the classic Christian teaching about sex is not homo-phobic – indeed, many same-sex oriented people believe it. Jesus calls us to love and accept everyone uncondi-tionally but to do so without compromising his teaching about sexual ethics. If you want to guide people, you first need to love them. But if you love someone, you will want them to grow in obedience to Christ.

What that looks like will vary from person to person, and will happen at different speeds. Gay people, just like everyone else, need to be assured proactively that we are loved and accepted just as we are. And when it comes to the speed at which our lives change after conversion, we need the same generosity and patience that the church already shows to plenty of other people.

Whether someone experiences any change in their sexual orientation or not, good pastoral care, prayer and in some cases responsible psychotherapy may offer someone a safe space to explore their feelings, accept themselves, and receive support. Fulfilled singleness should be seen as just as successful and legitimate a Christian goal as fulfilled marriage.

Whether someone chooses to identify themselves as gay or not does not automatically imply a view either way about sexual morality. For some people, identifying themselves as gay is an important step of self-acceptance. But the label can become a stumbling block, contributing to the experience of marginalisation and exclusion that many gay people feel. If so, some people may find it liberating to recover their physical sexual identity as their God-given reality, even if in a fallen world their sexual orientation does not fully line up with it. For some people, this change at the level of sexual identity may eventually lead to enough change in sexual feelings that marriage becomes a real possibility.

Opposite-sex-attracted people can help by avoiding labelling themselves as straight or heterosexual. This language reinforces the idea that straight is somehow 'normal' – whereas we are all equally fallen.

However, for most same-sex-attracted people, marriage has not become an option. Here, there is an urgent need for the church to recover and support a much more positive view of singleness as a fulfilling way of life (as I argue in *Sexual Singleness*). So having shown that the classic Christian teaching about marriage and sex has proven to be good and fulfilling in my own life as a gay or same-sex-attracted person, I look in depth at this teaching and the biblical reasons for it in *QUILTBAG: Jesus and Sexuality*, which I invite you to read next.

Go Deeper

True Freedom Trust (http://www.truefreedomtrust.co.uk/)

Andrew Goddard and Don Horrocks (eds.), *Resources for Church Leaders: Biblical and Pastoral Responses to Homosexuality* (London: Evangelical Alliance, 2012).

Wesley Hill, *Washed and Waiting: Reflections on Christian Faithfulness and Homosexuality* (Grand Rapids, MI: Zondervan, 2010).

Ed Shaw, *The Plausibility Problem: The Church and Same-Sex Attraction* (Nottingham: IVP, 2015).

Mark Yarhouse, *Homosexuality and the Christian: A Guide for Parents, Pastors, and Friends* (Bloomington, MN: Bethany House, 2010).

Some articles by Sean on the Living Out website

http://www.livingout.org/resources/how-should-i-respond-if-my-child-comes-out-to-me

http://www.livingout.org/resources/celibate-same-sex-couples

http://www.livingout.org/resources/becoming-christians-what-if-you-are-an-ssa-couple

http://www.livingout.org/is-it-ever-responsible-for-people-with-same-sex-attraction-to-get-married

ND - #0120 - 090625 - C0 - 198/129/2 - PB - 9781780781471 - Gloss Lamination